SPORTS
ALL-ST★RS

JUAN SOTO

Christina Hill

Lerner Publications ◆ Minneapolis

SPORTS THRILLS *MEET* RESEARCH SKILLS

Lerner SPORTS

Free Database Trial: **lernersports.com**

Lerner Publications Company
An imprint of Lerner Publishing Group, Inc.
241 First Avenue North
Minneapolis, MN 55401 USA

For reading levels and more information, look up this title at www.lernerbooks.com.

Main body text set in Albany Std. Typeface provided by Agfa.

Library of Congress Cataloging-in-Publication Data

Names: Hill, Christina, author.
Title: Juan Soto / Christina Hill.
Description: Minneapolis : Lerner Publications , [2022] | Series: Sports All-Stars (Lerner Sports) | Includes bibliographical references and index. | Audience: Ages 7–11 years | Audience: Grades 2–3 | Summary: "In 2019, nineteen-year-old outfielder Juan Soto helped the Washington Nationals win the World Series. Read about Soto's journey from the Dominican Republic to Washington, DC, and see what the future holds for the young superstar."— Provided by publisher.
Identifiers: LCCN 2021032445 (print) | LCCN 2021032446 (ebook) | ISBN 9781728441184 (Library Binding) | ISBN 9781728449418 (Paperback) | ISBN 9781728445144 (eBook)
Subjects: LCSH: Soto, Juan José, 1998—-Juvenile literature. | Outfielders (Baseball)—Biography—Juvenile literature. | Baseball players—Dominican Republic—Biography—Juvenile literature. | Washington Nationals (Baseball team)—History—Juvenile literature. | World Series (Baseball)—History—21st century. | Major League Baseball (Organization)—History—Juvenile literature.
Classification: LCC GV865.S59185 A3 2022 (print) | LCC GV865.S59185 (ebook) | DDC 796.357092 [B]—dc23

LC record available at https://lccn.loc.gov/2021032445
LC ebook record available at https://lccn.loc.gov/2021032446

Manufactured in the United States of America
1-49889-49732-7/15/2021

TABLE OF CONTENTS

WINNING
WALK-OFF

Juan Soto celebrates his game-winning hit against the Atlanta Braves on April 6, 2021.

On April 6, 2021, the Washington Nationals faced the Atlanta Braves. The game was Washington's season opener for the 2021 Major League Baseball (MLB) season. The two teams were tied 5–5 in the bottom of the ninth inning. Then Juan Soto walked up to the plate.

- **Date of birth:**
  October 25, 1998

- **Position:** outfielder

- **League:** MLB

- **Professional highlights:**
  helped the Washington Nationals
  win their first ever World Series
  in 2019; won the 2020 National
  League batting title with a .351
  average; hit his first career game-
  winning single in the first game of
  the 2021 season

- **Personal highlights:** grew up
  in the Dominican Republic with
  an older sister and a younger
  brother; nicknamed the Childish
  Bambino; loves to play
  video games

Soto swings at a pitch and crushes the ball.

At only 22 years old, it seemed that Soto had already done it all. He was a World Series champion. He had a long list of career highlights. But there was just one thing missing. He had never had a game-ending hit. In baseball, this is known as a walk-off.

Soto faced Braves pitcher Will Smith. The Nationals had runners on first and second base. After watching three pitches outside of the strike zone, Soto swung his bat hard at the fourth pitch. *Crack!* The baseball soared up the middle and into the outfield.

Soto's hit sent his teammate running from second to score the winning run. The game ended with a score of 6–5. Soto was named player of the game. His teammates cheered and hugged him as they celebrated the victory.

"It's my first walk-off in the big leagues," Soto said. "It's just amazing. Whenever I get to the plate, I just try to concentrate, try to hit the ball hard wherever it goes." It was a great win early in the season.

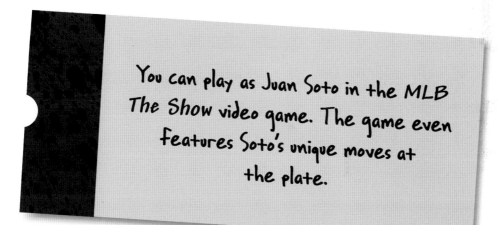

You can play as Juan Soto in the MLB The Show video game. The game even features Soto's unique moves at the plate.

TEENAGE
TRIUMPH

Juan José Soto Pacheco was born on October 25, 1998, in the Dominican Republic. He grew up in Herrera, a small city near the capital city of Santo Domingo. Juan has one older sister

Juan spent his childhood in the Dominican Republic.

and one younger brother. Like many kids, Juan spent his childhood years playing video games. He loved playing *MVP Baseball 2005* the most.

Juan's parents are his biggest fans. His mother, Belkis Pacheco, calls him "JuanJo" and cheers loudly during games. His father, Juan José Soto Sr., was a catcher in a local baseball league. Watching his father play sparked a passion for the sport in Juan. By the time he was old enough to play baseball, he was far better than the other kids his age.

Soto's talent was noticed by MLB scouts, and he signed a contract with the Nationals in 2015. He was only 16. Soto started on the Gulf Coast League Nationals, which is a team at the lowest level of the minor leagues. He earned the title of Gulf Coast League Most Valuable Player (MVP) his first year and was promoted to the next minor-league level. Over the next few years, Soto went from Low A to High A to AA. He played 122 minor-league games.

Soto runs around the bases after hitting a home run for his first career MLB hit.

In 2018, General Manager Mike Rizzo of the Nationals needed a new player. One of his outfielders was injured and unable to play. He decided to call Soto up to the majors. The move was a surprise to many fans. Soto was only 19. But his hard work and dedication to the game proved that he was ready.

Soto hits a home run against the Houston Astros during the 2019 World Series.

"If a guy's ready, he's ready," Nationals manager Dave Martinez said. "Doesn't matter his age. . . . I was just amazed at how mature he was in the batter's box."

Soto proved that age is just a number. In 2019, the Nationals faced the Houston Astros in the World Series. Soto started Game 1 of the series with a home run. He was the driving force needed to help the Nationals become World Series champions for the first time in team history.

Soto says that if he wasn't a professional baseball player, he would still work in sports. He would be a sports reporter.

LOVE OF
THE GAME

Soto celebrates a win in 2021.

Soto is a great baseball player because he loves the sport and wants to be at his best in every game. He is focused on eating healthful food and training hard.

13

Soto always works hard, even during pregame warm-ups.

Soto's teammates are impressed by his strict diet. However, he still loves to eat food he grew up with, including tamales.

Soto has a pregame routine that makes his coaches proud. Like many players, he believes that practice is key to his success.

Soto practices throwing before a game.

He never skips batting practice. Before every game, Soto runs through exercises that include hitting off a tee. He also watches videos of himself batting and the pitchers he will face that day. The hard work proves worthwhile in the batter's box, where he is ready to face any pitch thrown his way.

Soto wears a mask to prevent spreading
the virus that causes COVID-19.

When the disease COVID-19 spread around the world
in 2020, gyms shut down and people stayed home to
stop the spread of the virus that caused it. Soto posted
a video on Twitter that reminded people to be healthy,
wash their hands, and stay home. He also challenged
people to continue moving their bodies to stay in shape.
Soto said, "Stuck at home…no problem! I challenge you
to stay as safe, healthy, and fit as I am during these
tough times."

Soto partnered with sports equipment company Under Armour and posted a workout video that fans could follow from home. The video showed Soto working out in his garage. He focused on his stomach, chest, and back muscles with sit-ups, push-ups, and pull-ups. He lifted weights to strengthen muscles throughout his body.

Although Soto is young and healthy, he has battled a few injuries. While playing in the minor leagues, Soto broke his ankle. He also broke a bone in his hand. During his recovery time, Soto went home to the Dominican Republic. But he didn't let his time away from baseball get him down. He rested and healed his body and returned to the field better than ever.

As a teenager, Soto spent two hours every day learning the English language. He wanted to be able to speak English with reporters in the US.

FAN
FAVORITE

Soto takes time to sign balls and other baseball gear for young fans before and after games.

Soto is always smiling and having fun on the baseball field.

Despite his serious attitude about diet and exercise, Soto is full of energy and playfulness. On August 4, 2020, Soto's new teammate Josh Harrison hit his first home run for the Nationals. While his teammates cheered, Soto climbed

Soto (left) cheering with teammates Victor Robles (center) and Adam Eaton (right)

on top of the dugout to dance. His teammates laughed as Soto spun his arms and moved his feet in celebration.

Soto got used to life in the United States quickly, but he still misses things from the Dominican Republic. He especially misses the food. Soto's favorite meal is the popular Dominican dish *pastelón de plátano maduro*, or lasagna with plantain. A plantain is a fruit similar to a banana.

On October 2, 2019, Soto's family traveled to Washington, D.C., to watch him play in a playoff game. Soto's mom cooked his favorite meal. That night, he smacked a hit to right field that scored the winning run. Nationals fans hope that Soto's mom will cook for him before all of his big games.

Lasagna with plantain is made with sweet-tasting plantains instead of noodles.

Soto spends his time off the field working with charities. In 2020, the Step Up to the Plate campaign raised money to help families in the Dominican Republic who were suffering from the spread of COVID-19. Soto joined the cause and helped raise over $550,000. This money provided healthful food for families in need. It also helped provide medical supplies for hospitals.

Fans display their love for Soto with colorful, creative signs.

Soto is also taking part in a special video game event where fans will bid to join a team of famous baseball players. The teams will play together online. The top four teams will earn money for people in need. Charity groups such as No Kid Hungry, YMCA, and Pros for Heroes will benefit from the event. Fans on the winning team also get signed gear from the players.

Cover Model

Soto was chosen as the face of the 2021 Topps Baseball Cards collection. That means he appears on the front of all of their 2021 baseball card packs. A Topps official said, "As a young talent, World Series champion, and exciting player to watch, Juan is a great representation of today's game and was an easy choice for this year's cover athlete!"

Soto is the cover athlete for Topps baseball card packs.

The 2021 collection is special because Topps is celebrating their 70th year of selling baseball cards. Trading and collecting baseball cards is a popular pastime for many sports fans. Soto was happy to be a part of baseball card history.

o walks through
e dugout after a
ame against the
ew York Yankees.

In 2020, Soto won the National League batting title. He had the best batting average in the league at .351. Part of his success might come from his moves at home plate. Soto says he tries to get the

Soto smashes the ball for an RBI
against the Houston Astros.

attention of pitchers with his Soto Shuffle. First, he crouches down low. He then moves around in a strange dance. Soto says the rhythm of his movement helps him hit and distracts the pitcher.

The Soto Shuffle is an example of his fun-loving spirit. Soto's playful energy and powerful hitting earned him

Soto celebrates a win with Nationals manager Dave Martinez.

the nickname the Childish Bambino. The nickname started after Soto hit two home runs against the New York Yankees. One of New York's greatest players was the legendary hitter Babe Ruth, known as the Great Bambino.

Soto is still in the early stages of his baseball career, but he has already earned a Silver Slugger Award. Soto won this honor in 2020 for being the best hitter at his position. Due to COVID-19, MLB shortened the 2020 season. Soto had only 196 plate appearances in 47 games. He finished with 54 hits, 13 homers, and 37 RBIs.

"I definitely think you haven't seen the best of Juan Soto yet, that's for sure," Dave Martinez said. "He's going to continue to get better in all aspects of the game. You're talking about not only a potential MVP this year, but for many, many years."

When Soto was 10, his father told him that someday he would play in the World Series on his birthday. The prediction came true. Soto played in Game 3 of the 2019 World Series on his 21st birthday.

All-Star Stats

Major League Baseball Network (MLBN) creates the MLBN Top 100 Players list at the start of every season. Experts at the network rank players based on their stats, skills, and how the experts expect the players to perform in the future. In 2020, Juan Soto ranked 10th on the list. Here's a look at the top 10 players for 2021.

2021 MLBN Top 10 Players

1. Mike Trout   Los Angeles Angels

2. Mookie Betts   Los Angeles Dodgers

3. Jacob deGrom   New York Mets

4. Freddie Freeman   Atlanta Braves

5. Juan Soto   Washington Nationals

6. Fernando Tatis Jr.   San Diego Padres

7. Ronald Acuña Jr.   Atlanta Braves

8. Anthony Rendon   Los Angeles Angels

9. Christian Yelich   Milwaukee Brewers

10. Cody Bellinger   Los Angeles Dodgers

Glossary

batter's box: the rectangular area on either side of home plate in which the batter stands while at bat

batting average: a figure found by dividing the number of official times at bat into the number of base hits

dugout: a shelter on the side of a baseball diamond where players and coaches sit

minor league: a pro baseball league that is not a major league

plate appearance: a batter's turn at home plate

RBI: short for run batted in, a run in baseball that is driven in by a batter

scout: someone who judges the skills of athletes

tamale: cornmeal dough rolled with ground meat or beans and steamed

walk-off: ending a baseball game immediately by causing the winning run to score for the home team in the bottom of the last inning

Source Notes

7   Patrick Reddington, "Juan Soto's Walk-off Winner Last Night was the First Walk-off Hit of His MLB Career," *Federal Baseball*, April 7, 2021, https://www.federalbaseball.com/2021/4/7/22371160/washington-nationals-juan-soto-swinging-3-0-walk-off-winner.

12   Jamal Collier, "Nationals Call up Soto, Youngest Player in MLB," *MLB.com*, May 19, 2018, https://www.mlb.com/nationals/news/nationals-call-up-teenage-prospect-juan-soto-c277498492.

16   Jessica Camerato, "No Gym, No Problem! Soto Shares Home Workout," *MLB.com*, March 31, 2020, https://www.mlb.com/news/juan-soto-shares-home-conditioning-workout.

23   Stephen G. "Ghost" Mears, "Topps Picks Juan Soto for the Cover of their 2021 Series 1 Boxes and Packs," *TalkNats.com*, February 1, 2021, https://www.talknats.com/2021/02/01/topps-picks-juan-soto-cover-2021-series-1-boxes-packs/.

27   Keyln Soon, "With Disappointing Season Over, the Nationals Face an Offseason of Change," *Washington City Paper*, September 28, 2020, https://washingtoncitypaper.com/article/379045/with-unexceptional-season-over-the-nationals-face-an-offseason-of-change/.

Learn More

Buckley, James, Jr. *It's a Numbers Game: Baseball*. Washington, DC: National Geographic Kids, 2021.

Flynn, Brendan. *Washington Nationals All-Time Greats*. Burnsville, MN: Press Box Books, 2021.

Juan Soto
https://www.mlb.com/player/juan-soto-665742

Monson, James. *Behind the Scenes Baseball*. Minneapolis: Lerner Publications, 2020.

Postseason History: World Series
https://www.mlb.com/postseason/history/world-series

Washington Nationals
https://www.mlb.com/nationals

Index

Photo Acknowledgments

Patrick Smith/Staff/Getty Images, p.4; Patrick Smith/Staff/Getty Images, p.6; Cliff Welch/Icon Sportswire 357/Newscom, p.8; Walter Bibikow/Getty Images, p.9; Greg Fiume/Stringer/ZUMA Wire/Getty Images, p.10; Tim Warner/Stringer/Getty Images, p.11; Patrick Smith/Staff/Getty Images, p.13; Harry How/Staff/Getty Images, p.14; Greg Fiume/Stringer/Daily Express/Hulton Archive/Getty Images, p.15; Greg Fiume/Stringer/Getty Images, p.16; Christian Petersen/Staff/Philadelphia Inquirer/MCT/Getty Images, p.18; Rob Carr/Staff/Atlanta Journal-Constitution/TNS/Getty Images, p.19; Patrick Smith/Staff/Getty Images, p.20; ALLEKO/Getty Images, p.21; Patrick McDermott/Stringer/ZUMA Wire/Getty Images, p.22; John J. Kim/Chicago Tribune/Newscom, p.23; Michael Reaves/Stringer/Getty Images, p.24; Elsa/Staff/Getty Images, p.25; Mark Goldman/Icon Sportswire 749/Newscom, p.26

Cover: Robb Carr/Staff/Getty Images